PRESIDENTS OF THE U.S.A.

JAMES EARL CARTER
OUR THIRTY-NINTH PRESIDENT

by Lori Hobkirk

THE CHILD'S WORLD ®

The Child's World

Published in the United States of America

The Child's World®
1980 Lookout Drive • Mankato, MN 56003-1705
800-599-READ • www.childsworld.com

Acknowledgments
The Child's World®: Mary Berendes, Publishing Director

Creative Spark: Mary McGavic, Project Director; Melissa McDaniel, Editorial Director; Deborah Goodsite, Photo Research

The Design Lab: Kathleen Petelinsek, Design; Gregory Lindholm, Page Production

Content Adviser: David R. Smith, Adjunct Assistant Professor of History, University of Michigan–Ann Arbor

Photos
Cover and page 3: The Bridgeman Art Library International: Private Collection, Peter Newark American Pictures

Interior: Associated Press Images: 8, 14, 19 (Tomas Van Houtryve), 26 (Bob Daugherty), 35 and 39 (Gregory Smith); Corbis: 10, 16 (Owen Franken), 15, 22 (Corbis), 17, 25, 27, 28 (Bettmann), 34 (Mark Peterson); Getty Images: 9, 12 and 38 (Bernard Gotfryd), 11 (Hulton Archive), 21 (Karl Schumacher/Stringer/AFP), 24 (Getty Images), 30 (Emmanuel Dunand/AFP), 32 (Chris Hondros), 36 (Steve Schaefer/AFP); The Image Works: 33 (Michael A. Schwarz); iStockphoto: 44 (Tim Fan); Jimmy Carter Library: 4, 5 and 38, 6, 7; Photo Researchers, Inc.: 31 and 39 (Thomas S. England); U.S. Air Force photo: 45.

Library of Congress Cataloging–in–Publication Data
Hobkirk, Lori.
  James Earl Carter / by Lori Hobkirk.
     p. cm. — (Presidents of the U.S.A.)
  Includes bibliographical references and index.
  ISBN 978–1–60253–067–6 (library bound : alk. paper)
  1. Carter, Jimmy, 1924–Juvenile literature. 2. Presidents—United States—Biography—Juvenile literature. I. Title.
  E873.H625 2008
  973.926092—dc22
  [B]
                                        2007049025

Jimmy Carter served as president from 1977 to 1981.

TABLE OF CONTENTS

THE EARLY YEARS

James Earl Carter, the 39th U.S. president, insisted on being called "Jimmy," even as president. Jimmy Carter was born October 1, 1924 in Plains, Georgia. He first became involved in politics—the work of the government—as a young boy. His father, also named James Earl Carter, belonged to the Democratic Party, which is one of the country's two major political parties. A political party is a group of people who share similar ideas about how to run a government.

James Earl Carter was a peanut farmer, just like his son would be one day. He also owned a farm supply business. He sold tools and other items to local farmers. From his father, Jimmy learned to work hard. He also learned to take an interest in government and the farm's business. His father took young Jimmy to political barbecues throughout the Georgia countryside. At these events,

Jimmy Carter grew up on a farm in Plains, Georgia.

James Earl Carter Sr. with three of his four children. The future president is on the right. Jimmy Carter was close to his father. "He was the center of my life," Carter once said.

Jimmy Carter was the first U.S. president born in a hospital.

guests spent the whole day listening to politicians give speeches. They exchanged political talk and enjoyed barbecued pork and chicken. Little did anyone know that Jimmy would one day become the nation's most important leader.

Jimmy's mother, Lillian, was intelligent and open-minded. She always listened to Jimmy's ideas. She taught him to care for the poor. Together, Jimmy's parents encouraged him to learn about the U.S. government and to stand up for his beliefs. Many times in his life, people challenged Jimmy's ideas about what was right and wrong. But he stuck to his beliefs.

Jimmy Carter grew up in a home without electricity or running water.

As a young boy, Jimmy Carter won an award at school for reading more books than any other student.

In 1941, Jimmy graduated from Plains High School. He attended Georgia Southwestern College and later the Georgia Institute of Technology. In 1943, he was accepted into the U.S. Naval Academy in Annapolis, Maryland. Attending the academy was an honor, and Jimmy worked hard to do his best. He graduated in 1946 with a degree in **engineering.** That same year, he married Rosalynn Smith, a young woman he knew from Plains. He soon began his career in the navy. After two and a half years, he began working as an engineer on submarines.

In 1953, Jimmy learned that his father was dying of cancer. Jimmy was the chief engineer of a submarine crew, by this time. He, Rosalynn, and their three sons had been living in Schenectady, New York, where

As a young man, Carter loved sports. In this photograph of his high school basketball team, he is the second from the left in the top row. At the U.S. Naval Academy, he ran cross-country and played football.

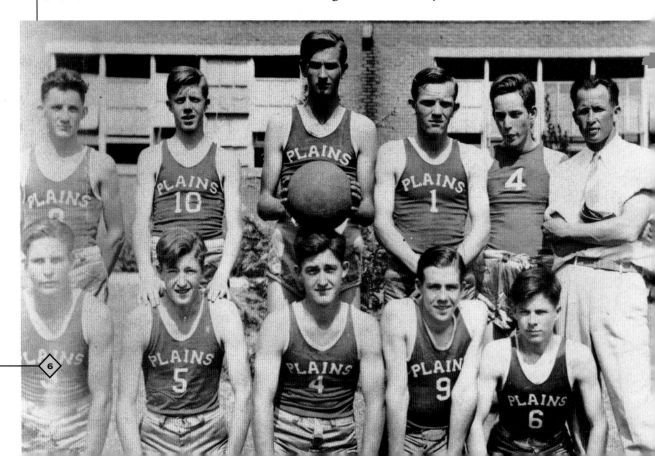

Jimmy Carter and Rosalynn Smith married the year he graduated from the U.S. Naval Academy. This is their wedding portrait.

Jimmy Carter was the first president to have graduated from the U.S. Naval Academy.

Jimmy was working on a new submarine. He was happy working for the navy, but he was faced with a difficult decision. After his father died, Jimmy wanted to help his family by supporting his mother in her old age and running the family farm and farm-supply business. He longed to return to the South. Finally, Jimmy decided that he and his family should move back to Plains.

Rosalynn was unhappy with his decision, but Jimmy's mind was made up. As always, when he made a decision, nothing stopped him. Leaving the navy would change the course of his life.

Right away, Carter set about improving the family business. He began planting peanuts from seeds at his farm. It took several years of hard work before the farm and supply business began to make a profit. "The entire first year I was home, our income was less than

Rosalynn and Jimmy Carter had known of each other for years before their first date. Rosalynn was a close friend of Jimmy's younger sister, Ruth. One day, Rosalynn saw a picture of Jimmy in Ruth's room. "I couldn't keep my eyes off the photograph," she later wrote. "I thought he was the most handsome young man I had ever seen."

Jimmy Carter ran a successful peanut farm. Here, Carter talks with his brother, Billy, in the family peanut warehouse.

$300," he later recalled. "But we stuck it out." Carter never had any doubt that he had made the right decision by going back home.

Rosalynn Carter helped run the business. At first, she worked only one day a week, but soon she was working full-time. In fact, she knew so much about farm supplies and peanuts that her husband often asked her for advice.

Meanwhile, their three sons—Jack, Chip, and Jeff—were growing up. (Their fourth child, Amy, would be born in 1967.) Carter became a leader at his local Baptist church. He also became involved with the local Lions Club, a service organization that does

charity work. In 1955, he ran for elective office for the first time. He was elected to the Sumter County Board of Education. He eventually served as its head for seven years.

In 1962, at age 38, Carter decided to run for the Georgia state senate so he could help make laws. Becoming a politician wasn't something Carter had ever imagined himself doing. But by this time, he had become interested in the state's education system and wanted to serve on the senate's education **committee.** Rosalynn supported his decision. In fact, she helped with the **campaign** whenever she could. She addressed letters, telephoned voters, and kept records. Carter won the election. He and his family moved to Atlanta, the state capital. It was the beginning of a long career in politics.

In 1966, Jimmy Carter's mother, Lillian, **volunteered** for the Peace Corps. She was 68 years old. The Peace Corps is an organization made up of volunteers who work overseas helping people in other nations. Lillian spent 23 months at the Godrej Colony in India, working as a nurse with people who had serious illnesses.

Lillian Carter worked as a nurse throughout Jimmy's childhood. She tended to poor people in the region, who would otherwise have received no medical care.

A CAREER IN POLITICS

In 1966, Jimmy Carter ran for governor of Georgia. He began the year running for a seat in the U.S. House of Representatives. But his Republican opponent dropped out and ran for governor instead. Carter did not want to see a Republican become governor of Georgia. So he dropped out of the race for Congress and ran for governor, too. He lost the election.

Carter spent the next four years preparing for another run for governor. He traveled tirelessly around Georgia, trying to understand the state's problems. He made more than 1,800 speeches. In 1970, Carter was elected governor of Georgia.

As governor, Carter made it clear that he would work to help all Georgians, especially those who most needed his assistance. "I say to you quite frankly that the time for racial discrimination is over," he said at his inauguration. "No poor, rural, weak, or black person should ever have to bear the additional burden of being deprived of the opportunity of an education, a job, or simple justice." His words drew the attention of people all over the nation.

By 1972, Carter was already considering the possibility of running for president. In September 1973, his mother asked him what he planned to do after leaving the governorship. Carter replied, "I'm going to run for president." "President of what?" she asked. "Momma," answered Carter, "I'm going to run for president of the United States, and I'm going to win."

CHAPTER TWO

AT HOME AND ABROAD

In 1976, the Democratic Party chose Carter as its **candidate** for president. Before the Democratic National Convention, Carter was thought to stand little chance of winning his party's **nomination.** He had been a peanut farmer and a little known governor. But being an unknown proved an advantage for Carter.

The nation was still weary from the Watergate **scandal.** The Watergate was a building where the national offices of the Democratic Party were located. In 1972, five men broke into the Democratic offices to steal important information. Leaders of the Republican Party wanted information about the Democrats' plans for the next election. It soon became clear that President Richard Nixon and his aides had been involved in the break-in and had tried to cover it up. In 1974, Nixon resigned in disgrace, and Vice President Gerald Ford became president.

When he ran for president, Jimmy Carter promised to restore the public's trust in the government.

Jimmy and Rosalynn Carter walk down the street with their daughter Amy on the day Carter became president. Carter was the first president to walk to the White House following his inauguration. Previous presidents had ridden in a carriage or a car.

Now, only two years later, many Americans welcomed a candidate who was not involved in the dirty politics of Washington, D.C. Accepting his party's nomination, Carter said that 1976 would be a memorable year "It will be a year of inspiration and hope," said Carter. "It will be a year in which we will give the government of this country back to the people of this country."

During the campaign, Carter emphasized human rights. Carter said it was a **privilege** to live in a **democracy** like the United States, where citizens influence how their government is run. In some nations, governments abuse citizens who speak out against their leaders. Carter believed the United States should not support any government that mistreated its people. Many Americans had faith in his plans. The 1976 election was very close, but Carter won, defeating Ford. He was the first southerner to be elected president since Zachary Taylor in 1848.

When Carter moved into the White House in 1977, many Americans knew little about him. Members of Congress also needed time to get to know the new president. Many considered Carter an outsider because he had not worked as a politician in Washington before he became president. They often made it difficult for him to reach his goals.

Even so, Carter had big plans. He wanted to protect human rights around the world. He wanted to improve educational opportunities for all Americans. He wanted to work for peace in the Middle East, the region where Asia, Africa, and Europe meet. There had long been conflicts among the diverse people who live in the Middle East. Carter believed the United States could help **negotiate** a peaceful solution to some of the region's problems.

Carter also wanted to reduce the number of nuclear weapons in the world. Both the United States and the Soviet Union, a large country made up of what are now Russia and other nations in eastern Europe and central Asia, had many of these weapons. One nuclear weapon can destroy a city and kill large numbers of people at one time. Carter hoped to negotiate an agreement with Soviet leaders. He wanted to reduce the risk that such weapons would ever be used.

The Carters' youngest child, Amy, was nine years old when they moved into the White House. Amy went to public school in Washington. She often brought friends home to play at the White House.

Global problems took up most of Carter's time. But the United States needed his attention, too. **Inflation** had been a major problem since Nixon's presidency. The prices of food, clothing, and other items were higher than ever. Many people in the United States could not find jobs. The nation's forests were being cut down, and pollution was harming the environment. The nation was in the midst of an energy **crisis,** so people had to cut back on how much gas and electricity they used.

Americans doubted that Jimmy Carter could fix everything that had gone wrong in recent years. It would have been a difficult job for anybody. But Carter wanted to tackle the problems his country faced. His way of doing this was to study every part of a problem before making a decision. Some people criticized him for this habit. They said it took him too long to act.

Jimmy Carter's vice president was Walter Mondale, who had previously been a senator from Minnesota. Mondale was an important adviser to President Carter. He was the first vice president to have an office in the White House.

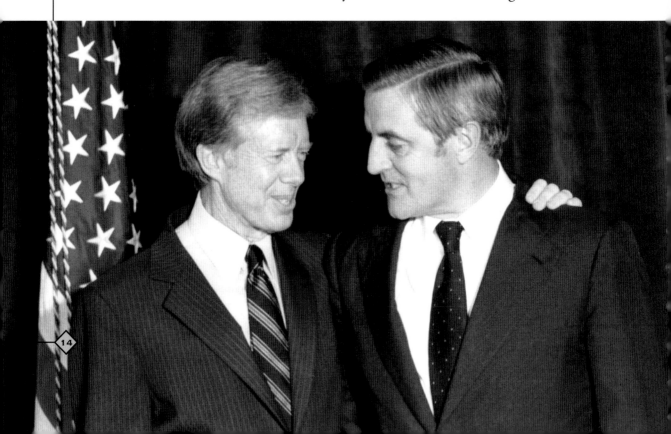

Rosalynn Carter took her role as first lady seriously. She understood and could explain her husband's position on every issue.

Still, Carter accomplished much with his dogged approach. He created the Department of Energy, which helped the nation use its energy sources more carefully. He worked to protect the environment. In 1980, he signed the Alaska National Interest Lands Conservation Act, which protected 104 million acres of Alaskan land. According to President Carter, signing this **bill** was one of the most satisfying acts of his presidency.

He also founded the Department of Education. He wanted more Americans to go to college. Expanding educational opportunities would help ensure that the country had a bright future. But many members of Congress didn't think the president should worry about education. As a result, it took almost three years to make the Department of Education a reality. Since then, the Department of Education has helped college students get loans that help them pay for school. The department also tries to improve public schools all over the nation.

When President Carter traveled around the United States, he preferred to stay in the homes of ordinary Americans instead of in expensive hotels.

Throughout his career, Jimmy Carter always asked his wife, Rosalynn, for her advice. When he became president, Jimmy and Rosalynn had a private meeting once a week to discuss political issues.

THE ENERGY CRISIS

The energy crisis was one of the most serious problems facing the United States in the 1970s. In 1973, the Organization of Petroleum Exporting Countries (OPEC), a group of 12 major oil-producing nations, cut the amount of oil it exported to the United States. OPEC was punishing the United States for supporting Israel in its war against neighboring Arab nations. With less oil available, the price of oil rose. There was also an oil shortage. Americans were afraid there wouldn't be enough gas to fill their cars' tanks. They waited in long lines at gas stations to buy expensive gasoline. Gas stations started to limit how much gas each person could buy.

The following year, OPEC began selling more oil to the United States once again, and the price of gas dropped. But many Americans believed they needed to find a way to use less energy. If they didn't, OPEC would have too much power over the United States.

Carter was determined to solve the energy crisis. He came up with an energy program and pressed Congress to support it. Congress finally passed a version of the bill 18 months after it was first introduced.

President Carter and his staff created the Department of Energy in 1977. This may have been one of his greatest achievements. Over the years, the department has worked to develop new energy sources. It has also encouraged Americans to carpool. Thanks to the Department of Energy, houses and office buildings are now built to use energy more efficiently. Manufacturers make appliances that use less energy. Carter's efforts to combat the energy crisis paid off. From 1977 to 1980, the amount of oil used in the United States dropped by 20 percent.

TREATIES FOR PEACE

President Carter devoted much of his time as president to problems outside the United States. Dealing with international issues was among the most challenging work of his career. Some Americans thought he spent too much time helping people in other parts of the world. They wanted him to solve problems at home first. But Carter wanted to help people wherever he could.

Soon after he became president, Carter began working on the Panama Canal **Treaty.** The Panama Canal is a waterway that cuts across the country of Panama, in Central America. The canal, which opened in 1914, was built to allow ships to pass between the Atlantic and the Pacific oceans. Before the canal was completed, ships had to travel all the way around the southern tip of South America. With the Panama Canal, the sea route from New York to San Francisco was shortened by 8,000 miles.

The United States built and paid for the canal. Since 1914, the United States had been in charge of it. But Panamanians wanted to run the canal themselves. Carter agreed. He believed it was the only way

to ensure friendly relations with the Central American nations. Carter and Panamanian leader Omar Torrijos Herrera agreed to a treaty giving control of the canal to Panama at the end of 1999. Many Americans were against the treaty. Still, President Carter was able to convince the Senate to approve it.

One of Carter's most important goals was to help promote peace between the nations of Egypt and Israel in the Middle East. It would be a difficult task. The creation of the nation of Israel in 1948 had left the Arab people of Palestine without a homeland. This angered both Palestinians and other Arabs in the region. They believed the Israelis had wrongly taken land that had belonged to Arabs for thousands of years.

In 1999, Carter attended a ceremony transferring control of the Panama Canal to Panama. Here, he exchanges documents with Panamanian president Mireya Moscoso.

19

A toll must be paid to pass through the Panama Canal. The highest toll ever paid was $249,165 by a container vessel. The lowest toll was 36¢. It was paid by Richard Halliburton, a man who swam the canal in 1928.

Over the course of 30 years, Arab nations and Israel fought five wars. As a result of these wars, Israel took control of more land that had once belonged to Arab nations. In particular, in 1967 Israel had seized the Sinai Peninsula, a stretch of land between Israel and Egypt. The peninsula had belonged to Egypt, and the Egyptians wanted it back. Israeli leaders refused to give it up and sent soldiers there to protect it.

Carter wanted to end the warfare in the region. He hoped to forge better relations not only between Israel and Egypt, but also among all nations in the Middle East. He decided the United States should help negotiate a solution. In 1978, he organized a **summit** at Camp David.

Camp David is a small complex located in the mountains of Maryland. It is a peaceful place where presidents can go for privacy and rest. Many presidents also hold important meetings there, because it is quiet and they can get much work done. Carter thought it was the perfect place to begin peace negotiations. He invited Egyptian president Anwar Sadat and Israeli prime minister Menachem Begin to Camp David. Carter was eager to greet the two leaders. He hoped to encourage a spirit of **cooperation.** He asked them to avoid arguments and angry words during their time at Camp David.

President Carter thought it would take three days to reach an agreement. But it would not come that easily. Begin refused to give back Egypt's land on the Sinai Peninsula. Sadat, angry, returned to his cabin

and packed his bags. Carter tried to persuade Sadat to stay, but Sadat refused. Finally, just as Sadat was about to leave for the airport, Begin agreed to return the land to Egypt.

After 13 days of long, difficult meetings, the leaders finally reached an agreement. They created the Camp David Accords, which were two separate plans. One plan outlined a peace treaty between Egypt and Israel. The other plan recommended ways to establish peace throughout the Middle East. The accords led to the signing of a peace treaty. Carter, Begin, and Sadat signed the treaty on March 26, 1979. It was a first step toward ending the ancient difficulties in this troubled region.

Egyptian president Anwar Sadat (left) shakes hands with Israeli president Menachem Begin during the Camp David summit.

In 1979, another part of the world demanded attention from President Carter. Carter and the Soviet leader, Leonid Brezhnev, had signed the Strategic Arms Limitations Talks (SALT II) Treaty earlier that year. Now the Senate had to approve it. This plan would reduce the number of nuclear arms that each nation produced. These weapons could cause terrible destruction. Carter hoped SALT II would reduce this risk.

Then, in late December 1979, the Soviet Union invaded Afghanistan. Afghanistan is located in central Asia, south of what was then the Soviet Union. The Soviet invasion created a serious problem. Americans feared that the Soviets were trying to expand their communist system to other parts of the world. Communism is a system in which a government controls the economy and owns most businesses. Most Americans believed it was dangerous and did not want it to spread to new places.

Carter knew that he had to show the Soviets that the United States did not approve of the invasion of Afghanistan. He asked the Senate to postpone its decision about the SALT II Treaty. Then he called for a grain **embargo** against the Soviet Union. The Soviets depended on the United States as a food source. The embargo meant that the United States would no longer supply them with grain.

Carter also withdrew American athletes from the 1980 Summer Olympic Games, which were being held in Moscow, the capital of the Soviet Union. This was among the most difficult decisions he made during his presidency. But the Soviets would earn a great deal of money by hosting the games, and Carter did not want to support them in any way until they removed their troops from Afghanistan. Other nations agreed with Carter's decision. In fact, 64 other nations did not send teams to the Olympics that year.

Unfortunately, Carter's efforts had little positive effect, and they actually hurt some Americans. The embargo hurt American farmers, who suffered because they sold fewer crops. American athletes who had trained for years for the Olympics lost their chance to compete in the 1980 Games. The Soviets did not leave Afghanistan until 1989.

Probably the most troublesome issue Carter faced during his presidency was the Iranian **hostage** crisis.

In 1978, Menachem Begin and Anwar Sadat won the Nobel Peace Prize for their work at the Camp David summit.

In January 1979, Iran's leader, Shah Mohammad Reza Pahlavi, had been exiled from his homeland. The word *shah* is an Iranian term for king. During the previous decades, Iran and the United States had been friendly. The United States provided the shah with military and economic aid. Iran provided the United States with a steady oil supply. Many Iranians did not support the shah's friendship with the United States. Finally, he was asked to leave his homeland. A religious leader, Ayatollah Khomeini (pronounced eye-yah-TOL-uh koh-MAY-nee), took over the Iranian government. Khomeini did not like the United States. Relations between the United States and Iran suffered.

*The shah of Iran (left) long had friendly relations with the United States. This angered many Iranians. They thought he was **corrupt** and objected to his lavish lifestyle.*

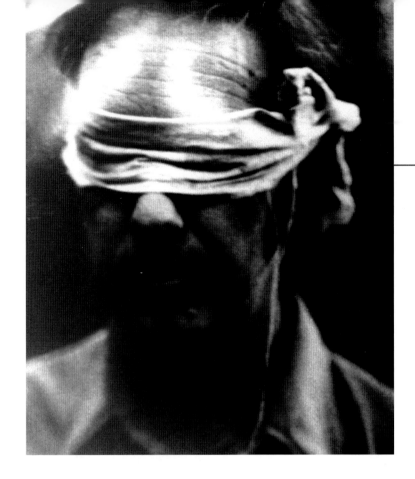

Americans were deeply worried about the fate of the hostages in Iran. All the hostages were eventually released.

The shah traveled to the Bahamas and then to Mexico, looking for a home. Then, he announced he had cancer and wanted to go to the United States for treatment. But Carter worried that this would harm America's already troubled relationship with Iran. He also hesitated because the shah had not always respected the human rights of Iran's citizens. Finally, Carter allowed the shah to travel to the Mayo Clinic, in Minnesota, for cancer treatment. In protest, a group of Iranian students seized the American Embassy in the Iranian capital of Tehran. They captured 66 American hostages. Fourteen hostages were soon released. The remaining 52 Americans were held hostage for 444 days.

Four years after the United States boycotted the Olympics, the Soviet Union refused to attend the 1984 Olympics in Los Angeles, California. Few other nations dropped out of the Olympics that year, however. Only 80 nations had competed in Moscow, but 140 went to Los Angeles.

A PEACE TREATY

The Camp David Accords led to an important treaty between Egypt and Israel that ended conflict between the two nations. President Anwar Sadat, President Jimmy Carter, and Prime Minister Menachem Begin (below, left to right) signed the treaty at the White House on March 26, 1979.

When countries sign a treaty, both sides promise to abide by certain agreements. Israel and Egypt agreed to a number of things. Israel promised to return Egypt's land on the Sinai Peninsula. It also promised to remove its military forces there. Egypt agreed to let the Israelis use its important waterway, the Suez Canal. Egypt also agreed to sell oil from Sinai to the Israelis.

Finally, Israel promised to begin peace negotiations with other Arab nations in the Middle East. The Israelis agreed to negotiations that would give the Palestinians more rights in the region, including the right to set up their own government.

A few days after they signed the treaty, Begin and Sadat met again in Cairo, Egypt (above). They agreed to set up a special telephone hotline so they could contact each other easily. Israel also planned to return part of Sinai to Egypt ahead of schedule. It seemed that the treaty had truly accomplished something. Perhaps peace in the Middle East was possible.

Not everyone approved of the treaty. Other Arab leaders still believed that Israel had no right to lands in the Middle East. And some Egyptians believed Sadat had given Israel more than it deserved. His enemies wanted to stop him from making further agreements with the Israelis. Sadat was **assassinated** on October 6, 1981. To this day, the Middle East still struggles for peace.

The hostage crisis made the last year of Carter's presidency difficult. In the spring of 1980, he approved a plan to rescue the hostages. On April 24, a secret helicopter mission was sent to Iran.

First, eight helicopters were to fly to Desert One, a location about 200 miles southeast of Tehran. Six transport planes would also fly to Desert One. The planes would carry fuel and other supplies. From there, the

In April 1979, Americans attempted to rescue the hostages in Iran. The mission failed when an airplane and a helicopter collided, killing eight of the rescuers.

helicopters would fly to the hills southeast of Tehran. But disaster struck at Desert One. As one of the helicopters was taking off, its propellers kicked up a huge cloud of dust. The pilot couldn't see through the dust, and the helicopter crashed into one of the transport planes. Eight Americans died in the accident.

The failed rescue mission only made relations worse between the United States and Iran. The shah died in July 1980, but this made no difference. Americans began to think that Carter had seriously mishandled the situation. The next election was coming up in November, and the hostage crisis hurt his chance of being reelected. On Election Day, Republican Ronald Reagan easily defeated Carter.

Later in November 1980, Iran sent a message to the United States. It had a list of conditions for the hostages' release. Carter worked on negotiations until the moment President Reagan took office. An agreement was finally announced on January 19, 1981, the day before Reagan's inauguration. The American hostages were released six minutes after Ronald Reagan became president, on January 20, 1981. Although it was Jimmy Carter's efforts that eventually freed the captives, many Americans gave the new president credit for solving the crisis.

On January 21, President Reagan sent Carter to meet the hostages at a U.S. military base in Germany. It was an emotional event for everybody involved—including the former president who had struggled so hard to win the hostages' freedom.

For recreation, Jimmy Carter enjoys fly-fishing, woodworking, jogging, cycling, tennis, and skiing.

Carter teaches Sunday school and is a deacon in the Maranatha Baptist Church in Plains, Georgia.

CHAPTER FOUR

AFTER THE PRESIDENCY

Carter's strong commitment to human rights did not end with his presidency. It would guide him in all future activities. Jimmy and Rosalynn Carter soon began to devote most of their time to helping people around the world.

Carter has remained active on the world stage since leaving the White House. Here, he is speaking at a conference in Asia.

In 1982, Carter became a professor at Emory University in Atlanta, Georgia. He enjoyed his work at the university, but he wanted to do more to help people. He realized that people in countries all over the globe lived in life-threatening situations caused by war, disease, hunger, and poverty. He believed he could find ways to help.

Jimmy and Rosalynn Carter soon founded the Carter Center. The goals of the Carter Center are to "prevent and resolve conflicts, enhance freedom and democracy, and improve health." Its vision is that everybody in the world should be able to live in peace.

The Carter Center is located near downtown Atlanta. One of the center's many goals is helping develop agriculture in poor countries. The Carter Center has helped more than one million farmers worldwide increase the **yield** *from their crops.*

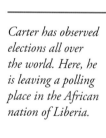

The Carters volunteer their time to Habitat for Humanity. Many people have become homeowners thanks to this organization. It offers loans to families in need so they can afford to buy a house. Each family helps build their own home, working with volunteers who offer their time and tools to the cause.

Several different teams work at the center. Some teams focus on helping nations build democracies. People from the Carter Center have observed elections in more than 20 countries, including Venezuela, Mexico, and Peru. By doing so, they have helped encourage free and fair elections. Representatives from the Carter Center have also negotiated peaceful solutions to problems in countries such as Sudan, Bosnia, and North Korea.

Some workers from the Carter Center fight disease. Others teach farmers how to grow more food for their families. Rosalynn Carter heads the center's program that aids Americans who struggle with mental illness.

Carter has observed elections all over the world. Here, he is leaving a polling place in the African nation of Liberia.

One of the Carter Center's biggest programs is called the Atlanta Project. It works to help people in Atlanta's most troubled neighborhoods. Health clinics and preschools have been built in these neighborhoods. The center also has after-school programs to give young people a safe place to go.

In addition to his work at the center, Carter has written many books since his presidency. Jimmy and Rosalynn have written a combined total of more than 20 books in nearly 30 years. Carter writes about topics that are important to him. He wrote a book on the history of the Middle East called *The Blood of Abraham* (1985). He also wrote a book called *Negotiation: The Alternative to Hostility* (1984). And he wrote a book about the environment called *An Outdoor Journal*

The Atlanta Project promotes education in Atlanta's poor neighborhoods. It also works to see that children in Atlanta receive good health care.

Jimmy Carter cuts a board while building a house with Habitat for Humanity. Jimmy and Rosalynn Carter have spent a week building houses every year since 1984.

(1988). He has also published books of poetry, fiction, and children's fiction.

His book *Palestine: Peace Not Apartheid* (2006) sparked controversy around the world. In this book, Carter discusses the persecution suffered by Palestinians living in areas controlled by Israel. His descriptions led some people to believe that Carter was anti-Israel. Carter explains that his aim was to present facts about the Middle East that were unknown to most Americans. He also wanted to restart peace talks, which he felt the United States had abandoned. He wanted these talks to lead to permanent peace for Israel and its neighbors.

In 2002, Jimmy Carter was awarded the Nobel Peace Prize "for his decades of untiring effort to find peaceful solutions to international conflicts, to advance democracy and human rights, and to promote economic and social development." The Nobel Committee specifically noted Carter's important contribution to the 1979 Camp David Accords between Israel and Egypt.

Just before he left office, Carter's White House staff presented him with a carpenter's tool set as a gift, knowing he enjoyed woodworking. The tools have come in very handy in Carter's work with Habitat for Humanity.

While he was president, Jimmy Carter worked to promote peace around the world. His efforts have continued since he left the White House. "We will not learn how to live together in peace by killing each other's children," he once said.

The Nobel Peace Prize is named after Alfred Nobel. Nobel was a Swedish inventor, most famously of dynamite. When Nobel died in 1896, he left most of his money to establish the Nobel Prizes. They are given every year for outstanding work in medicine, economics, physics, literature, chemistry, and peace.

Carter was the third U.S. president to receive the Nobel Peace Prize. The first two were Theodore Roosevelt and Woodrow Wilson.

Many people consider Jimmy Carter the nation's greatest former president. He has worked tirelessly to promote peace, human rights, and democracy around the world.

When Carter left the White House in January 1981, he promised himself that he would continue to be a world leader. He spoke the following words that would chart the course of the rest of his life: "The battle for human rights—at home and abroad—is far from over. We should never be surprised or discouraged because the impact of our efforts has had, and will always have, varied results. Rather, we should take pride that the ideals that gave birth to our nation still inspire the hopes of oppressed people around the world."

WAS CARTER A GOOD PRESIDENT?

No president escapes criticism, including Jimmy Carter. He accomplished many things during his presidency, but when he left office his popularity was at an all-time low.

During the summer of 1979, Carter's popularity turned from bad to worse. The energy crisis was in full swing. Gas prices were again skyrocketing, and there were long lines at gas stations. Of course, the public blamed the president for these troubles. People also felt that he had been unsuccessful in working with Congress to resolve the energy crisis.

In July 1979, Carter invited a small group of people to Camp David. This group was made up of political advisers, college professors, economists, and energy experts. They were people whom he deeply trusted. And he asked them for honest criticism of him and his presidency.

They told him that he was too bogged down in details and was not leading the country. They told him that he was involved in too many things and needed to **delegate** more. They were concerned that he would not follow through on plans and ideas. They also suggested that he replace many of his closest advisers. It was a harsh session, but many of their criticisms were true.

Carter sat on the floor and took notes. He was famous for taking extensive notes and studying issues in depth. For example, before his summit with Israeli prime minister Menachem Begin and Egyptian president Anwar Sadat, Carter studied volumes of books on each man. The information was about their lives, their childhoods, their families, and their likes and dislikes. He wanted to know every detail of their characters.

The session at Camp David with his advisers gave Carter a lot to think about. Perhaps it was possible to know too much about a certain topic. Perhaps his hunger for knowing all the details prevented him from actually governing. The next president, Ronald Reagan, was not known for paying attention to details or studying issues in depth. Yet he was more popular than Jimmy Carter.

What makes a good president? Is it knowing the issues inside out? Is it the ability to inspire the people? Or is it, perhaps, being willing to take a chance on a new idea, even if you're not sure it will succeed?

TIME LINE

1920 **1940** **1950** **1960** **1970**

1924
James Earl "Jimmy" Carter is born on October 1 in Plains, Georgia.

1927
Rosalynn Smith (Carter) is born on August 18 in Plains, Georgia.

1941
Jimmy Carter graduates from Plains High School. He enrolls at Georgia Southwestern College in Americus, Georgia, that fall.

1942
Carter transfers to the Georgia Institute of Technology.

1943
Carter is accepted to the U.S. Naval Academy in Annapolis, Maryland.

1946
Carter graduates from the U.S. Naval Academy. On July 7, he marries Rosalynn Smith.

1953
After his father dies, Carter leaves the U.S. Navy and returns to Plains. There, he runs the family business and peanut farm.

1962
Carter is elected to the Georgia state senate.

1966
Carter runs for governor of Georgia but loses.

1970
Carter is elected governor of Georgia.

1976
The Democratic Party nominates Carter as its presidential candidate. He runs against President Gerald Ford. Carter wins in a close election.

1977
Carter is inaugurated the 39th president of the United States on January 20. Carter establishes the Department of Energy. Carter and Panamanian leader General Omar Torrijos Herrera sign the Panama Canal Treaty.

1978

Carter hosts a summit at Camp David between Israeli prime minister Menachem Begin and Egyptian president Anwar Sadat. Carter hopes to negotiate a peace treaty. After 13 days of meetings, Begin, Sadat, and Carter agree to the Camp David Accords.

1979

The shah of Iran is forced from his country in January. Begin, Carter, and Sadat sign the Israel-Egypt Peace Treaty. Soviet leader Leonid Brezhnev and President Carter sign the SALT II Treaty. The Department of Education is formed. Student protestors storm the American Embassy in Tehran, taking dozens of hostages. The Soviet Union invades Afghanistan.

1980

The United States boycotts the 1980 Olympic Games in Moscow, the capital of the Soviet Union, to protest the Soviet invasion of Afghanistan. Carter and his advisers decide to attempt a rescue mission of the hostages in Iran. The attempt fails, and eight Americans are killed. Carter runs for reelection but loses to Republican Ronald Reagan. Carter signs the Alaska National Interest Lands Conservation Act.

1981

The terms for the release of the American hostages in Iran are negotiated during Carter's final days as president. The hostages are released shortly after Ronald Reagan's inauguration. Carter travels to a U.S. military base in Germany to welcome the hostages home.

1982

Carter is appointed professor at Emory University in Atlanta, Georgia. Jimmy and Rosalynn Carter found the Carter Center.

1991

Carter announces the Atlanta Project.

1998

The U.S. Navy names a submarine in Carter's honor. It is called the USS *Jimmy Carter*.

1999

Rosalynn and Jimmy Carter receive the Presidential Medal of Freedom. On December 31, a ceremony is held to turn the Panama Canal over to Panama.

2002

Carter wins the Nobel Peace Prize for his efforts to advance human rights, democracy, and economic and social development worldwide.

GLOSSARY

assassinated (uh-SASS-uh-nayt-ed)
Someone is assassinated if they are murdered. Anwar Sadat was assassinated in 1981.

bill (BILL) A bill is an idea for a new law that is presented to a group of lawmakers. Carter introduced a bill to help solve the energy crisis of the 1970s.

campaign (kam-PAYN) A campaign is the process of running for an election, including activities such as giving speeches or attending rallies. Rosalynn helped with her husband's campaign.

candidate (KAN-duh-date) A candidate is a person running in an election. Carter was the Democratic candidate for president in 1976 and 1980.

charity (CHAYR-i-tee) Charity is helpfulness towards those in need. Carter joined the Lions Club, which did charity work.

committee (ku-MI-tee) A committee is a group of people who work on a particular problem or issue. Carter wanted to serve on the education committee in the Georgia Senate.

cooperation (ko-ah-puh-RAY-shun) Cooperation is the act of working with others for everyone's benefit. Carter tried to encourage a spirit of cooperation at the Camp David summit.

corrupt (ku-RUPT) If people are corrupt, they act improperly for their own benefit, such as by taking bribes. Many Iranians thought the shah was corrupt.

crisis (KRY-sus) A crisis is an unstable or difficult time. Carter was president during the Iranian hostage crisis.

delegate (DEL-uh-gayt) To delegate means to entrust someone else to do a job. Carter's advisers told him he needed to delegate more.

democracy (deh-MAW-kruh-see) A democracy is a country in which the government is run by the people who live there. The United States is a democracy.

embargo (em-BAR-goh) An embargo is when one country stops selling a product to another country to make it agree to do something. During the grain embargo of 1980, the United States sold no grain to the Soviet Union.

engineering (en-juh-NEER-ing) Engineering is the science of building engines, machines, roads, and other things. Carter studied engineering at the U.S. Naval Academy.

hostage (HOS-tij) A hostage is a person held prisoner until some demand is agreed to. American hostages were held in Iran for 444 days.

inauguration (ih-nawg-yuh-RAY-shun) An inauguration is the ceremony that takes place when a new president begins a term. Carter's presidential inauguration took place in January 1977.

inflation (in-FLAY-shun) Inflation is a sharp and sudden rise in the price of goods. Inflation had been a problem for many years when Carter became president.

negotiate (neh-GO-she-ayt) If people negotiate, they talk things over and try to come to an agreement. Carter helped negotiate a treaty between Egypt and Israel.

nomination (nom-uh-NAY-shun) If someone receives a nomination, he or she is chosen by a political party to run for an office, such as the presidency. Carter received the Democratic nomination for president in 1976.

privilege (PRIV-lij) A privilege is a benefit or an advantage. Carter believes it is a privilege to live in a democracy.

scandal (SKAN-dl) A scandal is a shameful action that shocks the public. The Watergate scandal made Americans distrust the nation's leaders.

summit (SUM-it) A summit is a meeting of important government officials. The leaders of Egypt, Israel, and the United States held a summit at Camp David in 1978.

treaty (TREE-tee) A treaty is a formal agreement between nations. Carter negotiated many treaties with other nations.

volunteered (vaw-lun-TIRD) If someone volunteered, he or she offered to do a job, often without pay. Lillian Carter volunteered for the Peace Corps.

yield (YEELD) The yield is the amount of an agricultural product produced. The Carter Center has helped farmers around the world increase their yield.

THE UNITED STATES GOVERNMENT

The United States government is divided into three equal branches: the executive, the legislative, and the judicial. This division helps prevent abuses of power because each branch has to answer to the other two. No one branch can become too powerful.

EXECUTIVE BRANCH

PRESIDENT
VICE PRESIDENT
DEPARTMENTS

The job of the executive branch is to enforce the laws. It is headed by the president, who serves as the spokesperson for the United States around the world. The president signs bills into law and appoints important officials such as federal judges. He or she is also the commander in chief of the U.S. military. The president is assisted by the vice president, who takes over if the president dies or cannot carry out the duties of the office.

The executive branch also includes various departments, each focused on a specific topic. They include the Defense Department, the Justice Department, and the Agriculture Department. The department heads, along with other officials such as the vice president, serve as the president's closest advisers, called the cabinet.

LEGISLATIVE BRANCH

CONGRESS
Senate and
House of Representatives

The job of the legislative branch is to make the laws. It consists of Congress, which is divided into two parts: the Senate and the House of Representatives. The Senate has 100 members, and the House of Representatives has 435 members. Each state has two senators. The number of representatives a state has varies depending on the state's population.

Besides making laws, Congress also passes budgets and enacts taxes. In addition, it is responsible for declaring war, maintaining the military, and regulating trade with other countries.

JUDICIAL BRANCH

SUPREME COURT
COURTS OF APPEALS
DISTRICT COURTS

The job of the judicial branch is to interpret the laws. It consists of the nation's federal courts. Trials are held in district courts. During trials, judges must decide what laws mean and how they apply. Courts of appeals review the decisions made in district courts.

The nation's highest court is the Supreme Court. If someone disagrees with a court of appeals ruling, he or she can ask the Supreme Court to review it. The Supreme Court may refuse. The Supreme Court makes sure that decisions and laws do not violate the Constitution.

CHOOSING
THE PRESIDENT

It may seem odd, but American voters don't elect the president directly. Instead, the president is chosen using what is called the Electoral College.

Each state gets as many votes in the Electoral College as its combined total of senators and representatives in Congress. For example, Iowa has two senators and five representatives, so it gets seven electoral votes. Although the District of Columbia does not have any voting members in Congress, it gets three electoral votes. Usually, the candidate who wins the most votes in any given state receives all of that state's electoral votes.

To become president, a candidate must get more than half of the Electoral College votes. There are a total of 538 votes in the Electoral College, so a candidate needs 270 votes to win. If nobody receives 270 Electoral College votes, the House of Representatives chooses the president.

With the Electoral College system, the person who receives the most votes nationwide does not always receive the most electoral votes. This happened most recently in 2000, when Al Gore received half a million more national votes than George W. Bush. Bush became president because he had more Electoral College votes.

THE WHITE HOUSE

The White House is the official home of the president of the United States. It is located at 1600 Pennsylvania Avenue NW in Washington, D.C. In 1792, a contest was held to select the architect who would design the president's home. James Hoban won. Construction took eight years.

The first president, George Washington, never lived in the White House. The second president, John Adams, moved into the house in 1800, though the inside was not yet complete. During the War of 1812, British soldiers burned down much of the White House. It was rebuilt several years later.

The White House was changed through the years. Porches were added, and President Theodore Roosevelt added the West Wing. President William Taft changed the shape of the presidential office, making it into the famous Oval Office. While Harry Truman was president, the old house was discovered to be structurally weak. All the walls were reinforced with steel, and the rooms were rebuilt.

Today, the White House has 132 rooms (including 35 bathrooms), 28 fireplaces, and 3 elevators. It takes 570 gallons of paint to cover the outside of the six-story building. The White House provides the president with many ways to relax. It includes a putting green, a jogging track, a swimming pool, a tennis court, and beautifully landscaped gardens. The White House also has a movie theater, a billiard room, and a one-lane bowling alley.

PRESIDENTIAL PERKS

The job of president of the United States is challenging. It is probably one of the most stressful jobs in the world. Because of this, presidents are paid well, though not nearly as well as the leaders of large corporations. In 2007, the president earned $400,000 a year. Presidents also receive extra benefits that make the demanding job a little more appealing.

★ **Camp David:** In the 1940s, President Franklin D. Roosevelt chose this heavily wooded spot in the mountains of Maryland to be the presidential retreat, where presidents can relax. Even though it is a retreat, world business is conducted there. Most famously, President Jimmy Carter met with Middle Eastern leaders at Camp David in 1978. The result was a peace agreement between Israel and Egypt.

★ *Air Force One:* The president flies on a jet called *Air Force One*. It is a Boeing 747-200B that has been modified to meet the president's needs.

Air Force One is the size of a large home. It is equipped with a dining room, sleeping quarters, a conference room, and office space. It also has two kitchens that can provide food for up to 50 people.

★ **The Secret Service:** While not the most glamorous of the president's perks, the Secret Service is one of the most important. The Secret Service is a group of highly trained agents who protect the president and the president's family.

★ **The Presidential State Car:** The presidential limousine is a stretch Cadillac DTS.

It has been armored to protect the president in case of attack. Inside the plush car are a foldaway desk, an entertainment center, and a communications console.

★ **The Food:** The White House has five chefs who will make any food the president wants. The White House also has an extensive wine collection.

★ **Retirement:** A former president receives a pension, or retirement pay, of just under $180,000 a year. Former presidents also receive Secret Service protection for the rest of their lives.

FACTS

QUALIFICATIONS

To run for president, a candidate must

- ★ be at least 35 years old
- ★ be a citizen who was born in the United States
- ★ have lived in the United States for 14 years

TERM OF OFFICE

A president's term of office is four years.
No president can stay in office for more than two terms.

ELECTION DATE

The presidential election takes place every four years on the first Tuesday of November.

INAUGURATION DATE

Presidents are inaugurated on January 20.

OATH OF OFFICE

I do solemnly swear I will faithfully execute the office of the President of the United States and will to the best of my ability preserve, protect, and defend the Constitution of the United States.

WRITE A LETTER TO THE PRESIDENT

One of the best things about being a U.S. citizen is that Americans get to participate in their government. They can speak out if they feel government leaders aren't doing their jobs. They can also praise leaders who are going the extra mile. Do you have something you'd like the president to do? Should the president worry more about the environment and encourage people to recycle? Should the government spend more money on our schools? You can write a letter to the president to say how you feel!

1600 Pennsylvania Avenue
Washington, D.C. 20500
You can even send an e-mail to: president@whitehouse.gov

BOOKS

Acker, Kerry. *Jimmy Carter.* Philadelphia: Chelsea House Publishers, 2003.

Carter, Jimmy. *Talking Peace: A Vision for the Next Generation.* New York: Dutton Children's Books, 1993.

George, Linda, and Charles George. *Jimmy Carter: Builder of Peace.* Chicago: Children's Press, 2000.

Sandak, R. Cass. *The Carters.* New York: Crestwood House, 1993.

Santella, Andrew. *James Earl Carter Jr.* Minneapolis: Compass Point Books, 2003.

VIDEOS

American Experience: Jimmy Carter. DVD (Hollywood, CA: PBS Paramount, 2000).

The History Channel Presents The Presidents. DVD (New York: A&E Home Video, 2005).

National Geographic's Inside the White House. DVD (Washington, DC: National Geographic Video, 2003).

INTERNET SITES

Visit our Web page for lots of links about Jimmy Carter and other U.S. presidents:

http://www.childsworld.com/links

Note to Parents, Teachers, and Librarians: We routinely verify our Web links to make sure they are safe, active sites—so encourage your readers to check them out!

INDEX